C000071958

Published by McNaughty Books, an imprint of John Napir Ltd
P.O.Box 3353. London N.1. 1SR.
© MVIM B.S.Randle.
Design by Niamh Lehane.

ISBN 1-898 505 020
Printed and bound in the E.E.C.

MᴄNᴀᴜɢʜᴛʏ Bᴏᴏᴋs

THE McIRISH BOOK
OF
LOGIC

Up and down faster boys! A big order for milkshakes has come in!

Written & Compiled by **Seamus O'Really**
Illustrations by **John Watson**

contents

An Irishman was listening to a ventriloquist who was telling jokes. After fifteen Irish jokes in a row he jumped up and shouted:-

"I'm fed up with all these Irish jokes, we're not as stupid as you think."

"Look," said the ventriloquist, "It's only humour. I've always thought the Irish had a good sense of humour."

"I'm not talking to you," said the Irishman, "I'm talking to the little fellow on your knee."

*i*ntroduction

As with all Irish joke collections, the sources are numerous - previous collections and oral traditions both here and overseas. It is remarkable how jokes and stories travel, much like the myths and folk stories used to travel in ancient times. The jury story on page 62 was apparently told by Al Capone about an Italian whilst the French tell such stories about Belgians, Western European Americans about Polish Americans, English South Africans about the Boers, and the Irish themselves about Kerrymen.

In the sense that the stories are about another race they are of course racist, in the same sense that a survey of the living conditions of an ethnic minority or a History of France is racist. Whether they are racist in the sense of showing the race to be stupid is doubtful. The essence of the stories is a type of lateral thinking or different use of language - a perverse logic which takes an ordinary situation and makes it extraordinary. In an age of banality to claim that a race has such an ability is more of a compliment.

Seamus O'Really 1994

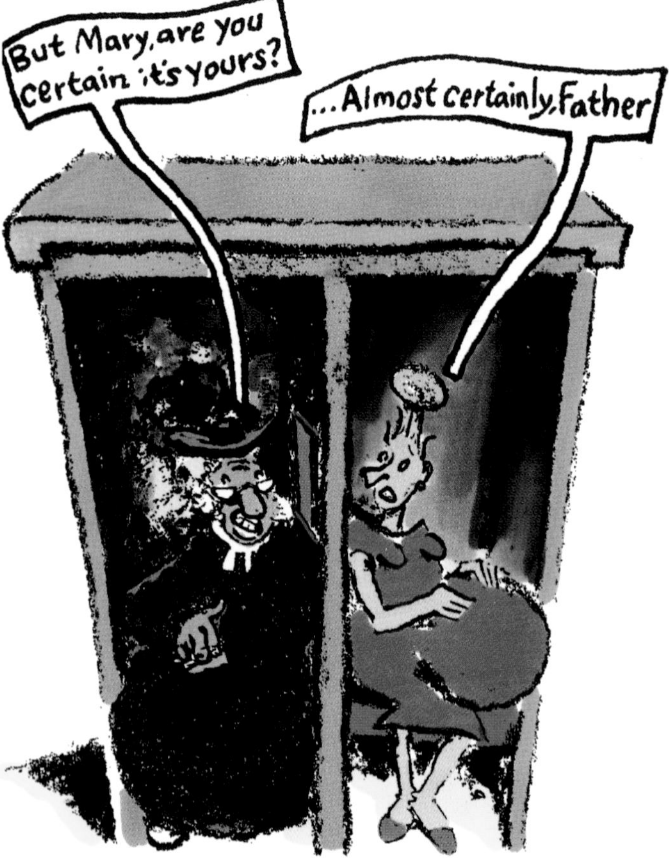
But Mary, are you certain it's yours?
...Almost certainly, Father

*a*rriving on earth

There's the old story of the pregnant Irish girl who confessed her situation to the priest.

"But Mary," said the priest, "Are you certain it's yours ?"

Mick arrived at the building site one morning proudly announcing that his wife had just given birth.

"I'll give you £5 if you guess what it is" he bet Paddy.

"A girl" Paddy replied.

"No, try again" said Mick.

"A boy" came the reply.

"Bejessus Paddy, how did you know that."

Mick lives on a remote farm with his chickens, his horse, two pigs, four cows, no electricity, and his heavily pregnant wife.

One day his wife goes into labour and Mick grabs a horse and sets off to find the doctor. Eventually they return after dark with Mick, holding the lamp, following the doctor into the bedroom.

"Mick," says the doctor, "Congratulations, it's a boy."

"That definitely calls for a drink," says Mick, turning to go to the kitchen.

"Just a minute, Mick, move the lamp over here" says the doctor "there's another boy."

Mick turns round and moves the lamp closer.

"And there's a third" cries the doctor.

"I don't mean to be superstitious at all," says Mick "but could it be that the lamp's attracting them ?"

●

Then there was an Irish woman filling out a form. The question of "sex" had two boxes: 'M' and 'F'. She ticked both and wrote "Sometimes on Saturdays too."

●

Up and down faster boys! A big order for milkshakes has come in!

*h*orses & farming

Q. How many Irishmen does it take to milk a cow?
A. Twenty, one to hold each teat, and 16 to lift the cow up and down.

Two pig farmers were talking one night over a drink in the pub.

"Tell me," said the first, "how is it that you get streaky bacon ?"

"Everybody knows that, you fool," replied the second, "you feed them and starve them on alternate days."

An Irishman was driving down a country lane one day when he saw a farmer struggling to pull a calf out of a cow. Only the calf's legs were showing. He stopped the car and went to give the farmer a hand, and an hour later, after much pulling, the calf finally emerged.

"How much do I owe you ?" asked the farmer.

"Oh nothing," came the reply, "but tell me how fast was the calf running when it hit that cow's ass?"

●

Mick was on holiday and decided to hire a horse for the day. When he got to the stables he chose his horse and saddled up.

"Just a moment," cried the stable boy, "you've got that saddle on back to front."

"Not necessarily," replied Mick, "you don't know which direction I'm going in."

●

Paddy sold a horse to Mick for £50, but thinking about it afterwards he thought that because Mick had not negotiated on the asking price the horse must be worth more. A week later he'd bought the horse back for £100. Then Mick got to thinking, and a week later he repurchased it for £150.

After a year the price had reached over £2600 when one week, whilst the horse was owned by Mick, he sold it to an American for £4000.

When Paddy heard, he went straight over to Mick's farm.

"You fool," he shouted, "why did you go and sell the horse - we were both making £100 a month on her."

●

Two Irish farmers were discussing the recent cattle auctions.

"Did you get as much as you were expecting for your cow ?" asked one.

"No. I didn't get what I expected," replied the other, "but I didn't expect that I would."

●

Mick and Joe each had a horse, but as they couldn't tell them apart Mick cut off his horse's tail. Unfortunately, soon afterwards, Joe's horse lost its tail in an accident and they were so confused they decided to ask the local priest for help.

"I don't see what the problem is, " said Father Mallone, "Surely you can see that the white horse is three inches taller than the black horse."

●

An Irishman bought a new horse, but everytime he put it into the stable its ears grazed the top of the doorway.

"I'll have to knock six inches out of the top of the doorway," he told his friend one day.

"Why not dig six inches out of the bottom," replied his friend, "It would be quicker and a lot cheaper."

"Ah no, it wouldn't work," came the reply, "It's the horse's ears that are causing the problem, not his feet."

Then there was the Irishman who claimed he had a rope with only one end - he had cut off the other.

●

An Irishman who has made a lot of money in the States as a ventriloquist returns to Ireland to look for a farm to buy. He finds one but the price is too high so he decides to use his skills to knock the price down.

Touring the yard he asks the horse "What's the barn like?"

"Needs a new roof," the horse replies.

The farmer looks very surprised and turns pale.

"What's the sty like?" the ventriloquist asks the pig.

"Hasn't been cleaned for weeks and the wood's rotten," replies the pig.

The farmer starts to shake. Next the cock starts to sing out.

"Holes in the wire, holes in the wire."

The farmer finally cracks, grabs the prospective buyer by the shoulder and says:-

"There'll be no need to be talking to the sheep - they all lie."

Q. How do you recognise an Irishman in a car wash ?

A. He's the one sitting on the horse.

One evening Paddy goes over to the drinks cupboard and finds the Scotch Whisky bottle empty.

"Have you been drinking all the whisky ?" he asks his wife.

"Oh no," she says "I've been giving it to the hens."

"The hens! Whatever for?"

"I'm trying to get them to lay scotch eggs."

●

Mick dropped round one day to see his neighbour Paddy. He found him in a field trying to make a cow drink its own milk from a bucket.

"Paddy what are you doing that for?" he asked

"Well Mick I thought the milk looked a bit thin, so I'm running it through again."

And then there's the joke about the Irish jellyfish.
It set.

●

ƒishing & shooting

Q. How does an Irishman catch a rabbit ?
A. He hides behind a tree and makes a noise like a lettuce.

Two Irishmen were out hunting one day when they saw a rabbit in the grass.

"Quick, shoot it" said one.

"I can't, I'm out of bullets" said the other.

"I know that, and you know that, but the rabbit doesn't."

Two Irishmen decide to go fishing. After much rowing they get to a spot where they catch ten fish

"This is great," said the first, "but how will we find this spot next time".

"No problem," said the second, "I've put a mark on the side of the boat".

"Bejessus, you idiot!" said the first, "what if we get a different boat next time."

●

Two Irishmen were out duck-shooting. They had their guns and dogs and walked for hours with no success. Dropping into the pub on the way back they listened with envy to all the other hunters who had obviously been very successful.

"Where d'you think we went wrong?" asked one.

His friend thought for a minute.

"You know I think it must be that we're not throwing the dogs high enough."

●

fishing and shooting

One day, strolling along the shore, Mick comes across an abandoned boat.

"Now," he thinks, "this'll do just fine for fishing."

Coming back an hour later with the fishing gear and Paddy his friend, he notices an old hole in one side of the boat.

"Don't worry," says Paddy, picking up a rock,

"I'll make a hole at the other side and then the water that flows in through the old hole, can flow out of the new hole."

●

Two Irishmen were out shooting ducks.

One took aim and hit a bird which tumbled out of the sky to land at his feet.

"Ah, you should have saved the bullet,"

said the other,

"The fall would have killed him anyway."

●

fishing and shooting

Two Irishmen were making plans for a Sunday fishing expedition.

"I'll pick you up at 2.pm." said the first.

"But what if it's raining in the afternoon?" asks the second.

"Why then I'll pick you up at 9.am !"

●

Two Irishmen out hunting one day realised that they were totally lost.

"Don't worry," said the first, "I know what to do; I'll fire three times in the air, and someone will come."

An hour later no help had arrived so he fired three times into the air again.

A further hour past.

"I think you'd better try again," said the second.

"Yes," said the first, "but it had better work this time, I'm almost out of arrows."

*b*uilding

Two Irishmen were constructing a house.
"Paddy", one called out, "we've got a problem
with the nails. The heads are on the wrong end."
"Don't worry", said Paddy, "those'll be for the other side
of the house."

The foreman is checking the work on a new house
when he comes across a broken window.
"This is no good, Paddy", he says, "this window's
cracked."
"Ah, I saw that myself", comes the reply "and you'll
notice it's cracked on the other side as well."

building

A man wanted his house redecorated and called in three builders for quotes. The first two quotes were high but Paddy seemed willing to do the job for almost nothing.

"How much for the living room?" he was asked.

"£50.27", replied Paddy, rushing to the window shouting

"Green side up, Green side up!"

"That's great, the others wanted £350; and how much for the bathroom?"

"£26.52", replied Paddy, rushing again to the window shouting

"Green side up, Green side up!"

"That's really good", said the houseowner, "the others wanted £250. You've got the job, but tell me what's all this business of shouting 'Green side up?'"

"Oh", replied Paddy, "that's technical information; you see my men are laying the lawn next door."

Q. How many Irishmen does it take to paint a house ?
A. Twenty-five. One to hold the paintbrush and twenty four to turn the house.

●

Two Irish companies were competing for a contract to put up telegraph poles. The authorities decided to test them, seeing which company could put up the most poles in an hour. The first company achieved twenty but when the second company's tally came in it was only two.

"I'm afraid you lost the job", the second company was told,

"the other boys managed twenty to your two."

"Ah", came the reply, "but they cheated, did you see how much they left sticking out of the ground?"

●

An Irish builder is showing a prospective buyer round a new house he's just built.

"Tell me," says the buyer, "Why does the bath have taps at both ends?"

"That's a special feature I installed", replies the builder.

"It ensures that the water is always level."

●

building

The Irishman had just finished building a really expensive house and was showing a buyer around.
"Tell me", said the buyer, "It looks great but why did you build it with three swimming pools?"
"Well the first one's for cold water for those who like a really invigorating swim, the second is for hot water for those who like it warm, and the third one's for leaving empty."
"Why the empty one?" asked the puzzled buyer.
"That's for your friends who can't swim."

●

An Irishman was digging a hole in a road when a passerby asked him what he was going to do with all the soil.
"Ah, well", he replied, "I'll dig another hole."
"But what if it doesn't all fit in?"
"Oh, I've thought about that," said the Irishman, "I'll dig the next hole deeper."

●

building

A passerby watched two Irishmen in a park. One was digging up holes and the other immediately filling them in again.

"Tell me", said the passerby, "What on earth are you doing ?"

"Well," said the digger, "Usually there are three of us. I dig, Paddy plants the tree and Mick fills in the hole. Today Paddy's off ill, but that doesn't mean Mick and I get the day off, does it ?"

●

T wo Irishmen were trying to have a nap on a building site. "I don't know how you can sleep on these pipes," said one, "they're terribly hard"

"Oh, I've solved that problem by stuffing them with straw."

●

An Irishman fell a hundred feet from a building site and was asked if he was hurt by the fall.

"Indeed not", he replied, "It wasn't the fall that hurt me at all, it was the sudden stop."

●

As the building site's office receptionist was ill, Paddy offered to stand in for the morning. The first call came through, the Irishman listened for a moment and slammed the phone down. "Who was that?" asked the manager. "Some idiot telling me it was a long-distance from Chicago. I told him everyone knows that."

●

An Irishman was working so hard on a building site carrying bricks up the ladder that his mate got worried. "What's up with you, working so hard?" he asked. "Don't worry," said the other, "I've got them all fooled, it's the same load of bricks each time."

Q. How do you confuse an Irishman ?
A. Put three shovels against the wall and ask him to take his pick.

●

*d*rinking & gambling

Mick has just learned a new party trick, and keen to show it to his friends he rushes into the pub.

"Paddy," he says, placing his hands on the bar, "pick a thumb, go on, any thumb."

Paddy obliges, whereupon Mick puts both hands behind his back and brings them out again as clenched fists.

"Now which one is it in ?"

About one o'clock in the morning after far too many drinks Mick is staggering around a lamp post, bashing it with his fists. Paddy comes across his friend and tries to help him to go home.

"Don't be stupid, Paddy, I can't move, I'm walled in."

Two tourists had heard how Irishmen can drink so they called an Irishman over and bet him £100 he couldn't drink twelve pints in ten minutes.

"O.K." said the Irishman, "but give me half an hour to get ready," and he left the pub.

Thirty minutes later he returned, got the landlord to line up the drinks on the bar and won the bet with seconds to spare.

"That was close," said one of the tourists, "we nearly won £100 off you."

"No chance," replied the Irishman, "I knew I could do it, 'cos I've just done it twice in the pub next door."

Q. How do you get £25 from an Irishman ?

A. Ask to borrow £50, then change your mind and say:
   "Look, just give me £25 to start with then you'll owe me the
   other £25, and I'll owe you the £25 I've borrowed, so we'll
   both be square."

●

Paddy felt he had been having just a little too much drink recently, so he decided to give the pub a miss on Mondays. The first Monday he forgot about his resolution but waking up with a hangover on the Tuesday vowed he would do better the following week.

He had almost got past the pub the next Monday when Mick called him in, and yet again he failed. The third Monday came and this time with superhuman willpower he passed the pub and kept going. A hundred yards down the road he thought to himself:-

"Congratulations, Paddy my boy, you've done it. Now that deserves a pint as a reward."

●

An Irishman goes into a pub with a sack over his shoulder
"Tell me," says his friend, "what's in the bag?"
"Ducks," comes the reply, "and if you guess how many there are I'll give you both of them."
"Five," replies his friend
"Bejessus, how did you know that!"

●

A group of Irish priests were holding a convention in a Dublin hotel, when the hotel manager was appalled to learn that they had just been served with watermelon spiked with brandy.

"Tell me," he asked the waiter "Have you had any complaints?"

"Ah no," the waiter replied "They're all far too busy sliding the seeds into their pockets to be doing any complaining."

●

Two Irishmen staggered drunk out of the pub and into the Pizza shop. One bets the other he can't eat a standard pizza in 60 seconds.

"How many pieces are there ?"

"Eight," replies the first.

"That's too many, get it cut into four and I'll take you on."

●

*t*he arts

The Irish girl left the convent and spent the summer holidays before going to University working in a trendy Dublin Art Gallery.

At the end of the summer she invited her mother to the opening of an exhibition of pictures painted by the owner of the Gallery. Her mother, looking at all the nudes, pulled her daughter aside.

"Mary," she said, "most of these nudes look very like you. You haven't been doing anything so sinful as posing in the nude have you?"

"Oh no," replied her blushing daughter, "he must have painted them from memory!"

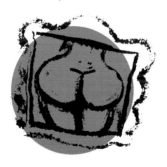

The Irish University football coach was complaining to a Professor how underpaid he was.

"But you make more than the whole History Department already," said the Professor.

"Maybe," the coach replied, "but you should see what I put up with."

"Watch this," he said, grabbing hold of one of his players who was passing.

"Sprint over to my office and see if I'm in," he told him.

Ten minutes later the player returned and after regaining his breath, duly reported "No sir, you're not there".

"I see what you mean," commiserated the Professor, "I'd have phoned."

Q. How do you keep an Irishman happy all day ?
A. Write P.T.O. on both sides of a piece of paper.

Hello, this is the professor... Am I there?
Just a minute, professor... I'll check....

Two Irishmen are sitting in front of T.V. watching a
cowboy film. Towards the end the bad guy is riding
furiously towards a cliff edge pursued by a posse.
"I'll bet you £20 that he jumps to his death over the cliff,"
says one.
"You're on," replies the second.
The bad guy rides over the cliff to his death.
The second Irishman hands over the £20.
"I feel a bit guilty," says the first,
"Because I've seen the film before."
"So've I," said the second, "but I didn't think he'd
be so stupid as to make the same mistake again."

●

A famous German orchestra arrived in Dublin to give a
concert. After the first rehearsal the conductor sought
out the stage manager and complained about the dreadful
acoustics.
"Ah, well I know," said the manager, "but what can I do. I've
even tried traps but I still can't get rid of them."

●

Immediately after the first act, Mick leaves the theatre and takes Mary to the pub.

"Why did you want to leave," says Mary, "Didn't you like it?"

"Don't be a fool," replies Mick, "Didn't you read the programme. The second act takes place two weeks later."

●

The Irishman was thrilled to receive a 16 piece jigsaw of the Statue of Liberty from his American nephew. Each day after work, he'd sit down with it for a few hours before going to the pub.

Finally he walked into the pub and proudly announced he had finished it and thought he'd apply to join Mensa.

"Mensa!" exclaimed his friend, "After taking three months to do a 16 piece puzzle".

"Ah, but the box says three to five years."

●

43

*i*rish abroad

An Irishman was lost in London so he asked a policeman where the other side of the street was. The policeman looked puzzled, but replied,"It's over there of course."
"I'm not surprised you look puzzled," said the Irishman, "I'm confused as well. I was over there a minute ago and some joker told me it was over here."

An Irishman on holiday in London decided to visit London Zoo. After visiting all the animals, following the signs to various cages, he spent half an hour looking for the Exit. Eventually he gave up, deciding it must have escaped.

Two Irishman are sitting on the docks in London when a couple of frogmen emerge.

"To be sure," says the first, "we should have thought of that, walked from Ireland and saved the fare."

●

Two Irishmen were on holiday in the United States and went up to see Niagara Falls.

Over drinks one night, one bet the other £500 he couldn't carry him across the falls on a tightrope.

After a very scary trip his friend managed to deposit him safely at the far end and the £500 was duly handed over.

"Pity," said the loser, "when you wobbled half way across I was sure I'd won."

●

And then there was the Irishman who congratulated himself on cheating Aer Lingus. He bought a return ticket, flew to London, and didn't go back.

●

An Irishman rang Aer Lingus and asked "How long does it take to fly to London?"

"Just a minute, Sir" came the reply.

"Thanks" said the Irishman and put the phone down.

●

An Irishman visiting London asked a policeman what time it was. "Five past Twelve," came the reply.

"This is a strange city," replied the Irishman, "I've been asking people all morning and I get a different reply each time."

●

After his first night at the hotel the Irishman came downstairs in the morning looking totally exhausted.

"I couldn't sleep at all" he complained to the manager.

"The blankets were too short so I spent all night cutting strips off the bottom and sewing them on the top. But, you know, the blankets are still too short."

●

Two Irishmen are flying home from London.
Shortly after taking off there is a big explosion and the pilot announces that one of the engines has gone and the flight will take 20 minutes longer Not long afterwards the pilot announces that a second engine has failed and the flight-time will be longer still. Half an hour later the pilot speaks to the passengers again to say that they are now flying on one engine and gives an even later arrival time. When the plane finally lands one Irishman turns to the other and remarks:- "Just as well the fourth engine kept going or we'd have been up there all night."

●

The hotel manager noticed in the register that one of his guests had signed XX.
He located the guest, an Irishman, who proudly informed him
"The first X stands for Michael O'Leary, and the second X for B.A."

●

tourists in ireland

An American tourist was boasting to an Irishman how advanced the Americans are.

"Gee, we've even put a man on the moon."

"That's nothing," replied the Irishman, "we're going to put a man on the sun."

"Don't be stupid," said the American, "he'll fry before he even gets there."

"Oh no, he won't, we're sending him at night."

A tourist dining in Ireland asked for coffee without cream. "Ah," said the waiter, "I can't get you that 'cos we haven't any cream. Would you mind if I got you coffee without milk instead?"

A tourist travelling in Ireland noticed that the village church tower had two clocks, but both showed a different time.

"Why the different times?" he asked a passerby.

"Well now, if they both showed the same time we surely wouldn't be needing two."

Two Irishman had filled the cart with hay and were driving it out of the field into the narrow road when a car came screeching down the road, jammed on its brakes and swerved into the field the Irishmen had just left.

"Thank the Lord," says one Irishman to the other

"We only just got out of that field in time."

A tourist was complaining about the roads in Ireland.

"Don't you have any plans for motorways?" he asked.

"To be sure," replied the Irishman, "but we've no plans to implement the plans."

*a*rmy & crime

An old Irishman is inside a bank when three bank-robbers burst in. After collecting the cash from the tills they turn on the customers, threatening to shoot them if they don't turn over their cash.
"I think you'd better shoot me then," said the old Irishman, "as I'll be needing my money for my old age."

And then there were the two Irishmen who hijacked a submarine, demanding a million pounds and two parachutes.

An Irishman joined the Irish Airforce dreaming that he would be an ace parachuter. When the time for his first jump came, the instructor told him:-

"Don't worry, jump out, count to ten and then pull the cord. If nothing happens the safety chute will open automatically. When you hit the ground the truck will be there to pick you up"

The Irishman jumped, but the chute failed to open and the safety chute failed as well.

"Bejesus," he thought, hurtling towards the ground, "I just bet the truck isn't there either."

●

Two Irishmen have been lying in wait for their enemy for over two hours.

Eventually Mick says " You know, he's very late. Bejesus, I hope nothing's happened to him."

●

Paddy and Mick decide to fight a duel but Paddy complains that Mick has an unfair advantage. "Look at the two of us," he says "I'm well over 20 stone and you are barely 8 stone. You've got a far bigger target" "I'll tell you what " replies Mick after thinking the matter over, "let's get a pot of paint and paint my shape on you. Any shots outside the paint won't count."

●

A one-eyed Irishman was challenged to a duel. He accepted provided he was allowed one advantage. "And what might that be?" asked the challenger. "Well, seeing as I've only got one eye, can I stand nearer to you?"

●

An Irishman decided to join the local police force and was asked to sit a written exam. He puzzled over all the questions until he came to the last one:- "Who killed Jesus Christ?"

On his return his wife asked how it had gone.

"Great," he replied, "I think they're putting me on a murder enquiry."

An Irishman had no idea his wife was having an affair, so he was mad with grief when coming home early one day he surprised her and her lover in the act. He grabbed a pistol and pointed it at his own head, which made his wife burst out laughing.

"What d'you think you're laughing at," he cried, "you're next."

And everyone's heard of the Irish terrorist who blew up a bus: he burned his lips on the exhaust pipe.

getting caught

The Englishman, the Irishman and the Welshman are arrested during the French Revolution. On conviction, they are all sentenced to death as spies, and told that they will be guillotined face up.

The Englishman is led out first, but after the order is given, the guillotine jams and he is set free.

The Welshman goes second and the same thing happens.

Finally the Irishman goes up, lies down and looks up at the guillotine.

"Hold it a moment," he shouts, "I think I can see what the problem is."

The Irishman was sentenced to be shot by firing squad.
"What will your last request be?" asked the officer,
"Nothing."
"Wouldn't you like a last cigarette?"
"Oh no," replied the Irishman, "I'm trying to give them up."

●

An Irishman was had up on a count of murder, so he
bribed his friend who was on the jury to return a
verdict of manslaughter.

The jury was out for eight hours before eventually returning
with the manslaughter decision.

Some weeks later the Irishman was visited in jail by his
friend and he congratulated him on his success.

"Ah," said his friend, "It was much harder than you think,
the other eleven wanted to acquit you."

●

Mick was describing the new judge to Paddy.
"He's thin" said Mick.
"How thin?" asked Paddy. "Well, I'm thin and you're thin,
but he's thinner than the both of us together."

●

An Irishman was charged with murder and pleaded
'Guilty'. The jury, to everyone's surprise though,
returned a 'Not Guilty' verdict.
The judge called the foreman over and asked him how a
'Not Guilty' verdict was possible.
"That's simple," replied the foreman, "We've all known the
accused for years, and none of us have ever heard a word
of truth out of him."

*And then there's the Irish kidnapper who enclosed a
stamped addressed envelope with the demand note.*

●

Paddy was called as a witness in a shoot out case but was proving a bit elusive on the witness-stand.

"Now tell me," said the judge, "Will you answer the question? Did you or did you not see the shot fired?"

"Well I didn't rightly see it, but I heard it," replied Paddy,

"That is not satisfactory," boomed the judge.

Paddy turned his back on the judge, winked at the accused, and started to leave the court, laughing.

The judge hauled him back and threatened to imprison him for contempt of court.

"Did you see me laugh?" asked Paddy.

"I've got ears, haven't I" shouted the Judge.

"That is not satisfactory."

*i*llness & death

One Irishman was explaining to the other how the Lord often compensates for a person's natural deficiencies.

"You see," he said, "If someone is a bit blind he might have a very good sense of hearing, or if his sense of taste has gone, he may have a keen sense of smell."

"You know," said the other, "I agree with you. I've always noticed that if someone has one short leg, the other is always just that little bit longer."

An Irishman's last wish was to be buried at sea, which was most unfortunate for his three friends who died digging the grave.

An Irishmans's father died so he decided to put a notice in the local paper. He phoned up the paper to find out how much it would cost,

"£25 per inch," came the reply.

"I'll never afford that," said the Irishman, "My father was 6 foot 2 inches."

●

The staunch old Catholic is lying on his death bed when he calls over a close friend.

"Mick," he says "you'd better fetch the Protestant vicar"

"What!" exclaims Mick, "After all these years as a Catholic surely you'll be wanting the priest"

"No Mick," comes the reply, "better for one of them to die than one of us."

●

It's always puzzled me, said the Irishman gazing up from his newspaper "how everytime the Lord gets it right. People always seem to be dying in alphabetical order."

●

An Irishman who had inherited a large sum of money from his American aunt went to the doctor with a badly injured arm.
"That looks very bad," said the doctor, "I'll have to give you a local anaesthetic."
"Oh, hang the expense," replied the Irishman, "I'll go for an imported one."

●

The Irishman went to the doctor, complaining that he had just lost his third job in three months.
"What appears to be the problem?" asked the doctor.
"Well I'm always late," replied the Irishman, "The trouble is that I sleep very slowly."

●

How badly is the soldier wounded? asked the Irish major. "Well," replied the doctor "To my mind there's no doubt that three of the wounds are fatal, but he's lucky that with the new medicines we now have, we should be able to cure the fourth."

●

Paddy had just turned fifty and he was concerned that his sex life was becoming non-existent.

So he went to the doctor who examined him.

"The main problem is that you're overweight, you smoke too much, you drink too much and you don't take any exercise," he said.

"Give up the drinking and smoking and run five miles a day and you'll find your sex life improves no end."

Surprisingly Paddy took the advice.

Three weeks later the doctor's phone rings. It's Paddy.

"How are you Paddy?"

"Never felt better," said Paddy.

"And how's the sex life?" asked the doctor.

"What sex-life?" said Paddy "I'm over two hundred miles away from home."

●

The doctor gives Paddy two weeks to live.

"Well, if it's alright with you doctor," says Paddy, "I'll have the first week at Christmas, and the second week in July."

●

McNaughty Books are available from all good
Book and Gift shops, or direct from the
publishers John Napir Ltd at P O Box 3353,
London N1 - 1SR at £4.99 per copy.